Finding Home

Finding Home
poems by
Mara Bright

Haley's
Athol, Massachusetts

© 2026 by Mara Bright.

All rights reserved. With the exception of short excerpts in a review or critical article, no part of this book may be re-produced by any means, including information storage and retrieval or photocopying equipment, without written permission of the publisher, Haley's.

Haley's
488 South Main Street
Athol, MA 01331
marcia2gagliardi@gmail.com
978.249.9400

Cover painting by Cindy White.
Copy edited by Debra Ellis.

International Standard Book Number, paperback:
 978-1-956055-44-3

Library of Congress Cataloguing in Publishing
 information pending

For Lila, Carina, and Parker

Your legacy is every life you touch.
—Maya Angelou

Contents

Simplicity   1
When Time Means Past and Future   2
Clay Speaks   4
Five Minutes with God   5
Conviction   6
Night Comes   7
By Design   8
When There Was Love   9
Starlings   10
Invitation   11
Refuge   12
What We Had Lost and Newly Found   13
Spring Fever in January Thaw   14
Conventions   15
Intervention   16
Season's Turning   17
Portable   18
Spring Comes Upon Us   20
Reluctant Parting   21
In the Estuary   22
Beauty's Bleakness without You   23
At Night Waiting   24
Tease   25
Come Play   26
Tree Reaching   27
Sanctuary   28
Cabin   29
The Early Years—Still Life   30
Heart's Cup   31
Itinerant   32
At the Channel   33
Mending   34
Wild Love   35
Sound Transforms   36

When Dancing Was the Food of Love   37
Tree   38
Shared Source   39
The Belonging   40
Sphagnum Morning at Julian's   41
What Do I Owe?   42
How Words Hide Us   43
Elegy for an Owl   44
Opening Wider   46
Ode to My 1993 Subaru Impreza   48
Practice   50
What a Day Brings   51
The Longing   52
Flow   54
Your Careless Words   55
When I Finally Let Go   56
Bodies Know   57
In the Manner of Billy Collins: I Forget My Hat   58
Early Morning Stillness on the Lake   59
Acknowledgments   61
About the Poet   63
Colophon   65

Simplicity

All morning I snip
tomato vines
from their cages
wrestle each free
mound the wilting greens
into my wheelbarrow

Started from seed
on my windowsill in February
delivered in May to their outdoor home
exploding in height and density
then overnight yielding up
their sweetness
as if their only
reason for being
is to teach abundance

Responding to sun
and rain and good dirt
generosity's envoys

When Time Means Past and Future

From an old Sierra Club calendar
I clip and glue a photo
on stiff paper to send
with greetings to a friend
on that page's back notations
from a week in a woman's life
my life in 1982

A dentist appointment
a walk with a friend
the phase of the moon—first quarter
Each day a fleeting miracle
never repeated twice
spent
collapsed into the next

Days stacked steadily into
something called a life
Hours like the rounded ends of logs
tawny in winter light
each resting on another
piled outside my window

What I feel is the bitter sweetness
of want while knowing there is no having
the longing to pause for a moment

in the unstoppable movement of days
knowing there is no stopping and
even now this moment
like all the others already gone

From the stillness of my deepest self
I see that time is not a line but
a long thrumming spiral stretching
in every direction at once
between here and there
yesterday and tomorrow
these words and my heart

Clay Speaks

Out of mud
a face a torso a family of souls
I pry clay from an arroyo's bottom
two days after rain
Restless to speak my hands work
rolling and flattening
pinching and fastening
receiving from earth's relaxed fist
the beginning of form

Some are shouting and clapping
the newly freed ones
while others blink silently
like lizards in the sun
We are you they flatter me
I am them

I lean their damp bodies against stones to dry
step back to regard each one
the one with arms flung wide
the mother hugging her chest
the seer
I turn away
leave their sun-dried shapes to erase themselves
in the next hard rain

Five Minutes with God

Diving for seeds under low shrubbery
juncos skate on crusty snow
They lift off and teeter
on the scalloped spikes of a stockade fence
one neighbor's declaration
of separation from another
in this suburban wasteland
where I don't expect to find life

And just as I write these words
I hear pecking against my window
emphatic and synchronous like
God's summoning of Moses
in the form of a fiery bush

Everywhere my senses land
is stroke after mysterious stroke
of God's paintbrush
One life

Most miraculous of all
I am
without even trying
part of it too

Conviction

While you are gone
I hold a space
in my mind for you
a clean white mindroom
for you

When our palms touched
we shed speech
our hands pressed
no words
I could not see your eyes
still our hands knew

My body has settled like a stone
tumbled to the bottom
of the river that is you
You ripple and sigh and
speak my name

In the white room
I light incense
drive out visitors
tear bread from a long loaf
and place it in your hands

Night Comes

You hills somewhere
in the dip and slide of you
lowland cradles swamp
keeps the peepers whose
twilight song bores through my skin
Darkness hangs its gauzy curtain
filters day through a sieve of threads
so fine that light flattens into shadow
and your subtle knots of color
blend into a single long scarf

What I want
is to be
in the dark with you
to light candles in the creases
of your brow

You hold the remnants of this day
in twilight's breath
In this last hour
I watch your shadows
gather into mine

By Design

Visible from Quabbin's shore
nine ducks navigate the inlet
dive together as one
leave no trace
their wild cries extinguished
beneath the water

Their presence ripples my heart
like the lake's surface
where now the egg-drop sun
floats on almost stillness

Bedeviled by brightness
sight seared and seeking shade
I turn away to umbrella myself
beneath a white pine

Already two hours past dawn
wind gets up
shoots through morning's gate
scours day with many tongues
tosses treetops
fans lake's skin

What does wind know
as it breathes through earth's lungs?
What do I know?

Nine ducks are at home
in the water

When There Was Love

I see you everywhere
your form imprinted
in chair cushions
your reflection in mirrors
that hang in my mother's house
your weight recorded
on her bathroom scale
In the shower's heat I heed
your desire for cool
and as I smooth white angelica
in body's furrows I wonder
have you adorned protection too
before you dance?

While I write you are dancing
Do you feel me close whenever
your attention strays from twirling?
Will you hold me in your arms
this night alone in our bed?
Is this what parting is?

You in me
my heart wide
as if you are here
and your eyes are tracking words
over my shoulder as I write them

I prepare to slip under sheets
in this other bed in this other house
See I leave a space for you
remembering to adjust my pillow
so
like this
I hear you
across the distance

You are laughing

Starlings

Roiling bird mass
accordion of shape heaving
in and out
in and out
a breathing paramecium
in flight
Who leads?
What increments of sight or
sound or movement
inform the rest?
This bellows pumping
sighing
What is it that senses
rhythm and glide
beyond leading
or following?

Could I reach my arm through
wear this streaming bracelet
around my wrist
a twirling pulse?

Pulse hugging pulse
a simple shared delirium
for flight

Invitation

I am waiting
for the sun
for a flash
through pine branches
glitter through glass

Clouds float backwards
as I float too
up my body's channel
an in-breath
then a breath I ride out
inside and outside continuous
still waiting for the sun
that is me and not me and brilliant

What in me watches
dives within for words
aches to give
sense's impressions speech?

Between experiencing and
the language for it
a gap
where the moment itself lives

An impulse to make plain the hidden
to uncover what is here all along
its root in my body
in sun and treetops

Refuge

You do not need to stay
awake far into the night
watching your breath and
turning over the hourglass
of your life

Love strings a hammock
across your door
slips pillows beneath your head
waits by you
until you sleep

In the bed you share
his arms fall across your chest
your head rests in the warm place
where neck and shoulder join
The magnets your bodies are
draw surely and
you fasten

What We Had Lost and Newly Found

Women claim your knowing
You have forgotten
You were the firekeepers
Her fierce gaze measures us
this emissary from our ancestors

She takes from her bag
a wooden bow and stick
rubs them together
From her belly she moves
pours intent through shoulder and arm
until friction births spark
With the remains from her bowing
she dusts the spark
carries the glowing orb outside
on a birch bark sliver

This nest will receive the spark
She nods toward the bundle
tucked in readiness
close to her heart

We have always done this
She blows gently
Fuel leaps into light
We gasp
Then clap
Initiates again

Spring Fever in January Thaw

May I be light
May I fling myself into air
again and again on trampoline
legs springboard soles
May I thrust myself up into night
shatter stars' stillness with singing
my heat spilling
into January cold

Boundless I am and air born
Given airtime I bounce
myself into being

Crazy woman
sprung forth from winter darkness
arms wheeling and gleeful
arrested finally and whole
sprawled on my back in
this trampoline cradle
heart noisy still jumping
Alive

I am calling stars yes
hanging whoops on the highest branches
I am grinning
myself lucent and bold

Conventions

In sun's pale time
when earth turns toward winter
I move through dark
feet crunching sand on pavement
jacket's nylon sleeves swishing
arms swinging with each step
brain registering walking

In the still six o'clock silence
holiday lights toss and wink
like stars saluting earth
from their outposts in heaven and
my mind records
the many sensations
of being
in this place

Time described by common agreements
accepted about material things
Feet connecting with pavement
"walking on streets"
these lights above me "stars"

This time the only
time I know
while I am earthbound
feet on pavement

In my human longing
I would unclasp mind's cloak
toss it from my shoulders
allow my soul wings

Intervention

On a ladder
picking beans green
with sun in my eyes
my small world brims

Looking up
I spy more pods
Four wave
their ripe fingers at me

With one more rung
to stand on
I wobble and stretch
snap each bean from
its vine alive
take from leafy plentitude
a docile harvest

My basket now
their home

Season's Turning

Reluctant to
release themselves
from dirt
dahlias come with me
after pulling
Tight tubers

In the season's turning
all-day-wind dashes
leaves to the ground
first frost's promise
I snip tubers from stems
set them on cardboard
to dry for winter storage

The last red blooms
rescued from wilting stalks
nod in a vase
Piled firewood rests
by the stove and
something stewy
simmers on top

A gathering-in close
against cold's coming
growth's denouement or
so it seems when
tucked dry and warm inside
chores done

Tomorrow I'll bag up
tubers store them
until spring
toss seed on the ground
for juncos

Portable

The smallest splinter exposed
like a tree root poking through ground
buried until yesterday
in my son's driveway
a rock taller than me and
broader than a tractor

Now newly delivered by backhoe
to an honorable place
above ground
it rests encased
in its dirt membrane

Reaching up I scrub
with a rake
metal fingernails scratching
rock's skin
Clay piles collect
at my feet

Poking and scraping
I dislodge more dirt
tear away lifetimes of
underground tenancy

The last stubborn crevices
yield to trowel and
rock ready for hose
I pronounce its baptism
Red rivulets run down its sides
and spatter my shoes

I ponder the lives of
things disinterred
or should I say
birthed like
pot shards or bones
pieced into a story
How little we know of
their past and yet
pretend authority

Spring Comes Upon Us

Spring comes upon us
like sap pooling
like maples budding
like love

We used to commune with
the spirits of animals
their tracks abundant
in the snowy forest

Once we spoke
to the souls of plants
and greeted the sun
in ritual salutation

No matter that we hover
in late winter
our connectedness forgotten
We are already attuned

The first mud and bird song
still take us

Reluctant Parting

Late September past equinox
first color
brushes leaves afloat
on Mattawa's surface
Still wet from swimming
I shiver when sun dips

Let me hold
the last of day's heat
like a stone in my hands

Setting it down
will mean
letting summer go

In the Estuary

Out of compacted mud
miniature canyons
wearing grass headdresses
bound the channels
we traverse at low tide

Shallow alleys absorb
September sun and
liquid salt drips
from our paddles

Sandpipers work shallow flats
and at the next divide
a blue heron levitates
plunges

We watch
in silence
drifting

Beauty's Bleakness without You

I carry you
on my skin on my shirt
Your scent clings
to my hair
even now as I bring
my body to this new place
soft Atlantic island

I watch from the shingle
as electrified swallows
dart above dunes
snare insects in midflight
as if to snag tendrils of
my soul which
still lingers with you
washes snow peas at your sink
pulls jewel weed
from your garden beds

You wait for me in another place
Me alive
there with you
struggle to attend
to clouds of barking gulls
rocks exposed by tide
wrapped in sea lettuce
the sudden fragrance of
beach roses red and white
on the roadside

I lean across miles into
the contours of your hands
They seek my face

At Night Waiting

Footsteps in the hall
on the stairs
in my head
Waiting in the late night
I am waiting
attuned to each sound
an engine's drone
a motor borne
on the ribbon of road
leading to my door

To know he is safe
A mother receives her son
in the deepest dark
when I would be sleeping
Instead I practice not caring
Not caring
he makes
his way
in the night
with his own eyes seeing

Tease

In this hybrid season
winter disguised as spring
budding forsythia restless
wrestles to stay asleep
Warm days beckon rain
instead of snow
January is a name

Skis snowshoes sled skates
wait indoors unused
My clock is set
to slowing
attuned to dark and coldness
I'm out of sync
in love with winter and
with this warmth
Caught

Can I really be complaining
a winter free of
frost on windshields
coaxing spinning wheels uphill
shoveling walks
throwing sand on ice?

I'm like a bulb prematurely stirring
forcing first shoots
upward through ground
I want to wiggle
strain closer to sun and
cocoon up
nestle deep under mountains of snow
Neither one fits
I fidget
Blame it on the weather

Come Play

The girl on the front steps
crushing yew berries into red paste
afraid of spiders
The girl crouching
at the top of the cellar stairs
overhearing secrets
The girl alone
waiting
for the rain to stop
for the big chair to relax its arms
and let her out
to play
but only when the sun is high

Too late too cold too dark

She stays deep in the chair
afraid to stir
careful not to hurt
to ask too many times
to betray her mother knowing best
by walking across the room
to where the day calls
through the closed door

Tree Reaching

At twilight by the river
greedy branches rake winter sky
Cold seeps up the bank
creeps under leaves
slides between rocks
crabs upward along bark
How many winters, tree?

Above the river's hungry roiling
branches scrape
needles sigh
They whisper to stones
in the language of tree and
river and wind
Will you speak to me, old one?

I would grow roots
meet you underground
slip into river
ride upon ice
tree song in my throat
touch your roots
where the deep water draws in

Sanctuary

She fashions cairns
on the shore
her stone ballet
She hears the keening
sounds the stones make
as the sea washes and
transmutes them

Seeking form
her hands
measure ballast
adjust lean
define her Stonehenge

She would practice mysteries
fill their stone lungs
with her own breath
so that they float
without her
on the dusk

Dumb masses of
acrobatic stillness

Cabin

A room of my own
adorned with what feeds me
stones and feathers
a rickety chair
seat softened with hand-weaving
braided rugs from woolen scraps
leftovers made whole

From the wall of windows
my eyes drift down the hillside
into gleaming woods
bare-leafed and newly washed
from yesterday's rain
Sun plays on laurel leaves
transforms them into
shimmering crystal
I perch on window's edge
lean out into the fine day
pull back to make more words
to give shape to my seeing

What if the moment dies unrecorded?
Does it go somewhere lost
the impulse to create
passed over in favor of other things?
The kindling box grown low
a letter to mail
a friend who needs calling

Stop

I walk eighty steps across the yard
to this haven
where each hour unravels itself
without calculation and
I remember myself
write myself whole

The Early Years—Still Life

Quite still
she observes life
from her chair
in the perfect
blue room
Caught whole
in the jaws
of the house
she grows smaller

And in the artificial light
she learns
to accept their pretty
ornaments and bright
careful talk
while days go by
and years
and she grows
smaller

The jaws of the house
clamp shut
Surely goodness and mercy

Still she sits alone
her trusting heart
waiting

Heart's Cup

I have fashioned a container
to hold my heart in
wild raging
hiding-behind-mountain heart

I light candles
speak holy words through smoke
gather dried blossoms
to drop into clay bowls

I would treasure heart's cup
cradle it in warm hands

I would breathe
into its rim

Like chaff floating upward
petals rise

And then and then
one hundred starlings burst
as one from their perch
on a wire
My heart a fisted bud
unfurls into light

Itinerant

Sodden snow exhales fog
silently corrodes
exposing layer upon layer of
cat leavings blow-downs
birdseed clustered pinfeathers
No different than any other organism
it decays
gases
liquifies
returns to solid earth

This snow corpse is barely a shade lighter
than the six o'clock March sky
which is the color of cement and
home to the wind
whose breath dries shreds of winter's wash
scours snow's last remains
transforms earth
into sweet mud

At the Channel

In the place where
channel cuts through marsh grass
gulls hover and dive for fiddler crabs

We wade to the farthest ingress
my daughter and I
and drop backwards into the tidal stream
two graceless sea creatures

Floating on our backs
we ride the current
christening clouds and
the wide day
until shallows beach us
Our laughter a soaring sea song

Applauded by gulls
streaming sand and sea water
we struggle up the shore
to ride the current again

Mending

My needle draws
in and down
followed by
up and out
catching threads
from warp and weft to
close fabric's rent
an apt word for
the ways we move
in the world
torn pieces
of ourselves

Sages say the cloth
is meant to tear
In each weaving live
the threads of imperfection
and demise
Still I dare to expect
the impossible
My needle's plodding
tells the story

When my hand's too
worn to mend
tomorrow's shirt
remind me of
acceptance then

Wild Love

Everywhere on this island Theodoroi where I spend three weeks on the edge of the moon, from every promontory, from every direction along the track leading to the abandoned chapel courtyard is the sea, the glistening Aegean, pulsing improbable blues and greens with every incremental shift of light. Shades to make a person weep, so varied and alive, until the fading light flattens blue into silver, silver into dove, and the sea lies like a pale cloth across a table between shores.

On this rock off Crete's southern strand, red earth, terra rosa, invades the microscopic crevices of my skin, seeps into my cells, tinges my arms and legs so that after ten days in the field and two soapings in the shower in Chania, the rinse water runs rusty, my clothes dyed with the rosy grit of red lunar hillsides.

Rock faces, pock-marked, exploded like sponges with enlarged pores, rough like barnacles to the touch, capable of ripping skin, slashing clothing, barely support the vegetation that grows here,
that thrives on desiccating winds without rain for six months at once, silvery foliage or none at all.

After midnight when we herd the last of the wild goats into our traps, the final weighing, measuring and sampling complete, we struggle down the ragged stone-strewn path to our camp to sleep for two hours before the heat of the sun bearing down on our tents evicts us.

We stumble to the platform shaded by tarps, our kitchen/laboratory, where one of us tests DNA from last night's blood draws. I cut cheese from the wheel, runny and soft from a week in the sun, and tear a fistful of bread from a basket suspended by ropes to deter Norway rats, the only other species of mammal here besides the goats.

I eat while looking out again at the sea, always and everywhere the sea, hot breeze already ruffling its surface, precursor to the sirocco, the angry North African desert wind that will that afternoon twist tent poles, rip canvas, throw us out upon the bare earth, terra rosa for my bones, and commence a series of nights where from my back I see above me millions of stars.

Sound Transforms

All day we gather
last year's garden leavings
cut brush
prune fruit trees
drag or carry limbs
to throw into the fire

Inside Bach's music
floats from the radio
filling the house
Baroque light and order ooze
like water into every nook and crack
seep behind plaster
under tiles
inside coffee cups
across stacked firewood
and tabletops
cling to cushions and plants

On sound's surface
float leaves pine needles sticks
sweet ornaments
on liquid continuo

We put down our rakes and go inside
How will we know the air is changed
made extraordinary
by all day receiving?
When we open our mouths
will we find new speech
our cells by sound waves rearranged?

When Dancing Was the Food of Love

In thick dark armed with boombox
CDs and swinging lantern
we dash across the street and
summoning invisibility circle
the town hall looking for
a door someone failed to lock
a way in
I strike a match
light the lamp
You plug in the music
schottisches mazurkas polskas hambos
each demanding a different
set of figures

I spin with you
around and around the room's perimeter
our faces lit by lantern
hands warming to the shuttered
inside cold
We practice for two winters
no one the wiser
united by a common secret
the dance's flowering
and the freedom of flying
around the whole hall
no one stopping us
until at last we fall
into each other's arms
breathless and laughing

We were lovers then
For that little while
I let you be a nest
for my heart

Tree

I follow you up mountains
along streams
into the territory
of my undeclared visions
unremembered dreams

Each season
your summons
sings me back to humbleness
for the small being I am
as you loom straight-trunked
and arcing above me

There is so little
to be afraid of in this world
Nothing really
I am never alone here
beside your
quiet immensity

Teach me to pray
as you do
arms outstretched
fingertips tracing sky's cheek
in complete
readiness and attention

Shared Source

I am only one more
who follows the track
carved by others long ago
It hugs the land's contours
skirts thickets of mountain laurel
and hugs a brook whose
rocky shelf I hop
to tread beyond

Other landmarks guide me
a topless beech
a stand of viburnum hobbled by deer
a downed white pine

My truest compass is
the hollows and uplands
the sudden hill I recognize that
erupts out of flatness
the gulley that holds glacial tumble

I know where porcupines build
their cities in ledges that
rise like fortresses
from the forest floor
I know where moose penetrate
an understory so thick
I must bob and bend to
creep through it
I follow their tracks
They let me be

I find my ground in these woods
our sameness

The Belonging

I conjure sugar maples like
the ones I passed this morning
marking the road that connects
two villages now erased
Ancient, still stalwart
bark tunneled by time
whose scabrous limbs gaunt as ghosts
reach like masts toward the sky
I wander the path between them
another presence like theirs in the forest

For two hundred years
they have communed underground
shared the day's news
traded recipes and the latest remedies
while all around the forest goes
about its business
Squirrels wave their tails
Finches searching for seed plummet
like rain to the ground

I tread fallen needles of white pine
buried rocks and wind-pruned branches
rambling with open eyes
limited only by my humanness

Sphagnum Morning at Julian's

Bench boards support my back
the ground my feet
Sun at October's apex spreads
Warm fingers across my face
No sound
Out of stillness
the faintest breeze brushes
my shoulder my neck and now
lifts a page of my notebook

All sensed through this *I* and
as if to announce her *I-ness* too
a finch erupts into song
her words a version of mine

What lives beyond sensing
sees beyond seeing
directs this hand to scribe
imagined truths?

What Do I Owe?

What do I owe the black-capped
chickadee whose presence again
animates my window at breakfast?
I may be the caster of seed she forages
but she is the author of
my swelling heart
For these moments we are linked
two multiplied by infinity
each other's abundance
my morning sweetness
her dessert

Our leaders in Washington
have forgotten their source
They too are dependent on the earth
They would erase their animal natures
deny that as denizens of this planet
they are bound to her imperatives and
to every other living being
whose home is here

Do they know a universe exists
beyond their stifling rooms of power?

Despite the chaos they rain down
the chickadee returns each morning
as each morning turns toward noon and
noon toward night

How Words Hide Us

Once we pleasured in
the way we fit like
smooth matched stones

Since we've come apart
we fashion words
to bind us
Would you like tea?
Please pass the salt?
Have you fed the cats?

Simple forms
they are jam on bread
Now they unravel
like threads dissipating into
a tangle of air

Our words hang like curtains in
an empty house

Elegy for an Owl

I

My graveled feet
tread the wet road
eyes tracking each rippling shadow
on bark and branch's tip
By a familiar oak I stop
adjust the scarf against my neck
There in the leaves
I spy a soft feathered heap
gasp in recognition
An owl petite
facing down and in
uncommon repose
I roll her to her back
Inspect her face
her tidy beak
her eyes' shuttered stare
Bending down I
bear her to road's edge
mound her with leaves
an impromptu burial

II

You saw-whet
eyes round and tender
tell me what you know about death
Did you summon me
to find you this way?

III
Winter let your snow-filled hands
sweeten her leafy grave
Bury her in deep white
Bless her nocturnal brightness
with your icy breath
She who knew the branches of hemlocks
and with her swivel head scanned
for mice in open places
Bless her curved beak and
fervent eyes
Delight in her mottled tail feathers
and since you cannot fill
her form with life again
gentle her body in spotless snow

Opening Wider

Do they slide on their bellies or backs?
I wonder bending over
shallow furrows etched in snow
That otters play in Mormon Hollow Brook
delights me
A few steps later I stop
confirm their tracks
follow them until mountain laurel
hopelessly dense bars me

Gaging the easiest route
I abandon thought
duck and plunge
certain that the path will open
as I go

On the other side I pause
unlace one boot
yank an errant sock slipped below my heel
swallow water
pick off sticks clinging to my hat
note the faint impressions left on snow
barely enough to follow

Not quite lost
I find myself somewhere
on a side of Bear Mountain unfamiliar to me
perhaps a mile from my door
yet here I am
enjoying the silence
alone

Though not really
An oak tree holds me where I lean
back molded against bark
Showered sunlight
warms my face
Parts of a sacred symbiosis
this moment and I
two halves of one holy wandering

Ode to My 1993 Subaru Impreza

Sprung whole like Athena from Zeus's head
you leapt already mine from the pages of *The Want Advertiser*
We closed the deal in a Friendly's parking lot
sedan of my dreams

I'd done the wagon thing
graduated from wife and full-time mom
You were my companion in danger
during my first post-divorce years
Together we dove into my singlehood

We commuted together too
on snow and ice
on wet pavement
on back roads through hills
shaded by hardwoods and hemlock

How many breakfast bowls of oatmeal have I consumed with you
while gazing through your windshield?
I steered
You carried us there
to the Guiding Star Grange for dancing
to the dump loaded with a month's recycling
to the Farmers' Coop for mulch hay

You doubled as a locker and kept at the ready
work boots and sneakers
a hoe and light shovel
roller blades towel bathing suit
and mat for massage
You understood the language of necessary surprises
a day's unexpected delights

You were my traveling altar
the bearer of stones and feathers
driftwood and polished glass

We made it up the steep hill to home most times in winter
you with your studded snows and determination
me with earnest urging
It was that last half mile that showed me your heart
With roaring engine pulling with all you had
you got us to the top
On nights you didn't
you kept us from slipping as I backed down the hill
and tucked you in at the pull-out below

As you aged your efficiency increased
your miles per gallon climbed and
I bragged about you to my friends
We were extensions of each other
Yesterday when the tears came
I lit candles for us to mark
the miles we traveled together
the hours we spent in each other's company

Another life begins for you in your twilight time
Fifteen years old and
more than two hundred thousand miles under your wheels
Another woman wants to drive you until you quit
As I pass her your keys
I ask her to love you

Thank you
steady stalwart friend

Practice

I note the simple act
of lifting
spoon to mouth
while eyes distracted
scan windows and wall

Forty-three degrees outside and
over there the utility pole
like the moonlit mast
of a lost ship
beams in the sun

I swallow my tea and
follow its swift
slide down my throat
a moment attentive
to sensation

Seduced by habit
my mind spins off
planning the day
put up bird feeder
dig dahlias
pick wild grapes for jelly

And now arrested by chewing
I stop
blueberry taste on my tongue

Tasting seeing sensing
mind registers eating
in this now

What a Day Brings

All night rain
wears away the snow pack
and everything is running
Watery pleats score earth's skin
and tumbling snowmelt trips
over itself on its way
downhill to the river

From the bridge I spy
a fisher uncoil the tight rope
of her body to
pad atop yielding snow

In rapt attention I watch

Upon waking today
I didn't expect
a fisher's presence
to brim my heart
in gratitude or
these words to spill like
runoff on white paper

The Longing

I want you to risk once
I want you to tear
dark muscle from
chest cage
Soak it in the cup
of your salt tears
until swollen and soft
the sinews fall like ribbons
into your hands

I want you to soothe
each strand with your
lover's touch
Cherish each
imperfect chord
Bring cup to lips
to taste heart's broth
the transmutation of
your walled heart made
whole again

I want to risk once
I want to tear
dark muscle from
chest cage
Soak it in the cup
of my salt tears
until swollen and soft
the sinews fall like ribbons
into my hands

I want to soothe
each strand with my
lover's touch
Cherish each
imperfect chord
Bring cup to lips
to taste heart's broth
the transmutation of
my walled heart made
whole again

Flow

You say everything dies in winter

Out in the woods on skis
my tracks stretch behind me
I stop to loosen my scarf
Wrapping me in their silence
the trees listen
I lean against my pole
with mittened fist
I hear the trees breathing
Birches and white pine
brush an agate sky
fine gray lines against a pale wash

You fear the cold
the long bitterness?

My skis hum across the surface of the snow
Waxed wood wings
they carry me home

Your Careless Words

... sting the soft skin
here on my cheek
You teach me
to weave a silent circle around you
like skirting a snake
by going the long way over rocks
Still I remark on its beauty

Or else I face you head-on
and risk the ruin of my words
against the fortress of you

You repel me
your strike finding hidden wounds
How raw I am and curled in
upon myself
bent by the swiftness
of your last rebuke

I carve your initials
in my flesh
Look they are here in my arm

When I Finally Let Go

Defrosting the freezer is
like melting armored layers of myself
I fill a pan with boiling water
let it sit inside
to work the ice
through steamy suggestion

Without mounting a defense
frosty deposits thick
give up
I scrape the loosened chunks
sponge away runoff

Blessed are the ways of transformation
the easy change in matter's state
Had I forgotten
every river finds its way
to the sea?
How foolish to resist

Mind too long chilly and wanting
too long afraid
reaches in vain to open

I welcome body's knowing
its gentle untwining
its trust

Bodies Know

Your shoulders tell the weather
by their tension
Let them ride easy
atop hips and legs
They know their connection
to the ground

Finding shelter
in these woods of oak and hemlock
your feet at home in their duff
let your body walk you

You used to think you could
wrestle pain into silence
blot out hurt
through words and
ceaseless doing

Let your shoulders drop their burden
like fall's fallen gold and yellow leaves
defending nothing and
resting unhurt on the forest floor

In the Manner of Billy Collins: I Forget My Hat

First a stick then
a sliver of grass clinging
to blueberries
I shake from a freezer bag
onto this morning's cereal
evidence of last summer
hatless in the blueberry field
my head melting
like a popsicle in the sun
droplets running
down my cheeks
no shade anywhere
bushes sizzling
stretched-in-the-heat berry skins
near bursting
greedy wasps on siesta
somewhere else

When to stop picking is
not even a question
That bush over there loaded
with berries begs for relief
Heavy clusters tip branches
to the ground

I approach my work seriously
More than taking and tasting is
my synergy with ripeness
a fancy thought that
distracts me from the sweat
dripping into my eyes
the sweet berry crush
on my tongue
the hat I wish I'd
remembered

Early Morning Stillness on the Lake

We slip off the dock and
disturb the clear surface
Our arms and legs reach
propel
crease the liquid plane
each stroke producing
such a clarity of sound within stillness
that the simple flight of a bird
readies the branch of a tree
on the other shore and
our words
carried on rings of air
are preserved whole
after we speak them

We haul ourselves up onto the dock
and sit dripping in the sun
while eating fruit and yogurt
out of pottery bowls
while clouds track soundlessly
moment eclipsed by moment
as sure as light shifts and plays
against the surface of the lake
as sure as our breathing

Acknowledgments

The idea for this book was born after Linda Chatfield, director of New Salem Public Library, invited me to do a reading of my poems for National Poetry Month. After the reading, an enthusiastic audience asked to buy my book, a book that didn't yet exist. Thanks to Linda and that audience for being the impetus.

With thanks as well to Sara Schley, my writing buddy for twenty-five years, who helped me decide on the title.

A big thank you to Cindy White for her cover art that expresses the reverence and delight we share for the natural world.

To Marcia Gagliardi, my editor and publisher, appreciation for her "getting me" and wanting to deliver a collection of poems true to my vision.

About the Poet

Mara Bright

Poet Mara Bright is a mother, grandmother, spouse, and friend. She's a former high school English teacher and school librarian who has facilitated writers' groups for adults for more than twenty years. She has written for *School Library Journal, Calliope, Cobblestone, Faces,* and local publications. Her early poems appear in *Bone Cages,* an anthology published by Haley's. She is the author of *The Constant Heart,* a memoir.

As a professional astrologer, she does readings and teaches astrology.

She loves outdoor adventuring, wandering in the woods, and playing in her gardens.

She lives in rural Western Massachusetts with her partner, a piano, and lots of house plants.

Colophon

Type and captions for *Finding Home* are set in the font Garamond, a group of serif typefaces named for sixteenth-century Parisian engraver Claude Garamond, generally spelled as Garamont in his lifetime. Garamond-style typefaces are popular to this day and often used for book printing and body text.

Garamond's types followed the model of an influential typeface cut for Venetian printer Aldus Manutius by his punchcutter Francesco Griffo in 1495 and in the twenty-first century called the old-style of serif letter design, letters with a relatively organic structure resembling handwriting with a pen but with a slightly more structured, upright design.

Following an eclipse in popularity in the eighteenth and nineteenth centuries, many modern revival faces in the Garamond style have since been developed. Although Garamond himself is considered a major figure in French printing of the sixteenth century, historical research has increasingly placed him in context as one artisan punchcutter among many active at a time of rapid production of new typefaces in sixteenth-century France, and research has only slowly developed into which fonts were cut by him and which by contemporaries.

Many Garamond revivals of the early twentieth century are based on the work of a later punchcutter, Jean Jannon, whose noticeably different work was for some years misattributed to Garamond.

Finding Home titles are set in the font Arial, a sans-serif typeface in the neo-grotesque style. The typeface was designed in 1982 by Robin Nicholas and Patricia Saunders for Monotype Typography. It is metrically compatible with Helvetica, enabling documents to use either typeface without affecting the visual layout. Because of their similar appearance, Arial and Helvetica are commonly mistaken for each other.

www.ingramcontent.com/pod-product-compliance
Lightning Source LLC
Chambersburg PA
CBHW040312050426
42450CB00020B/3464